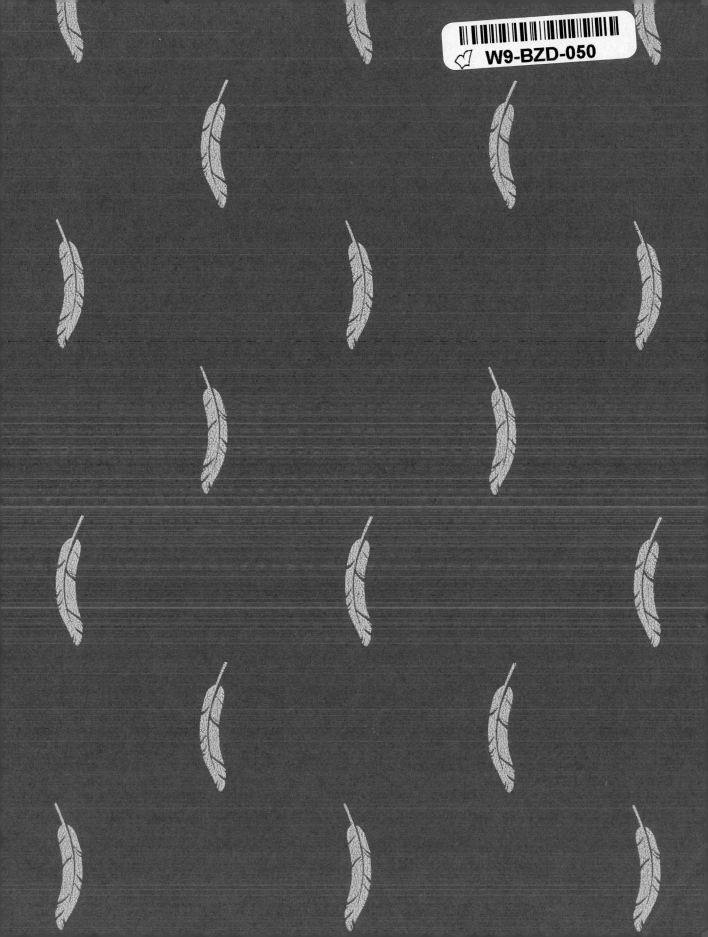

S W A N
L A K E

Mark Helprin

Illustrated by Chris Van Allsburg

Ariel Books

Houghton Mifflin Company

Boston 1989

Library of Congress Cataloging-in-Publication Data

Helprin, Mark.
  Swan Lake/Mark Helprin: illustrated by Chris Van Allsburg.
    p.   cm.
  Summary: A young prince and his beloved Odette struggle against the
evil Von Rothbart to protect themselves and their infant
daughter in this adaptation of the classic ballet.
    ISBN 0-395-49858-9
    [1. Ballets—Stories, plots, etc. 2. Fairy tales.] I. Van
Allsburg, Chris, ill. II. Title.
PZ8.H3697Sw   1989   89-31269
[Fic]—dc19   CIP
                          AC

Text copyright © 1989 by Mark Helprin
Illustrations copyright © 1989 by Chris Van Allsburg

Printed in the United States of America

H 10 9 8 7 6 5 4 3 2 1

List of Illustrations

For Alexandra and Olivia

M.H.

Once, the mountains held within their silvered walls a forest so high and so gracefully forgotten that it rode above the troubles of the world as easily as the blinding white clouds that sometimes catch on jagged peaks and musically unfurl. Cold lakes scattered in the greenery ran so deep that soundings were of no avail, and the meadows along the tree line, suspended in the light, were as smooth and green as slabs of jade.

Here birds sought refuge from hunters on the plain, and found higher realms in tranquillity and perfection. And though empires and kingdoms below might nervously claim it, the forest was in its own way inviolable — a domain of hearth smoke in unwavering columns against a flawless blue sky, of mountains clad in wind-buffed ice, of the thinnest air, of rivers running white and bursting with oxygen.

Perhaps you have felt the presence of such places when, in a darkened concert hall, the music makes the moon rise, perfectly fresh and bright, as if the roof has opened up above you, or when the trees shudder in a sudden wind and the sun unexpectedly lights the undersides of their rustling leaves. They do exist, although they are so hard to find that it is tempting to believe they are illusions. But all places cannot be exactly the same. Some are slightly better than others; some are much better; some are vastly better. Were the world uniform, you would not be able to distinguish a pin from a needle. But you can, of course. And what about a pin and a hippopotamus? And that is just the beginning. As for those who would deny the existence of forests hidden in a crown of mountains, of sheltered places, of charged landscapes that can put together broken hearts, or at least keep them from shattering into pieces, ask them about hippopotamuses and pins.

The forest was a place of exile for an old man and a little girl. She believed that her mother and father were still on the plain below, caught up in struggles she could hardly imagine. Though she did not remember them, she loved them, and had just reached an age when she wanted, most of all, to join them.

Because the old man understood that she knew little but her childhood, he thought to tell her something of the world that she was determined to see.

This was long ago, and in many ways the time was so different that you would hardly know it, except in your heart — for your heart is quick and right to tell you that all things that matter are more or less the same as they have been and will be, and that however young you are, however happy you may be, somehow you know them, somehow you know sadness; somehow, you have been there.

The old man often told the little girl stories as she lay in her bed in a tiny room lined with fragrant cedar. Stories had been something to dream upon. But this one was for the full light, and he wanted to tell it, and did, on a late summer afternoon when the roses were hot and completely unbound, and the hay stood in dry blonding sheaves.

They had been working since dawn. They were exhausted. Never had she questioned the hard labor, winter or summer, and she had always risen and retired with the sun. But he had known girls, with eyes just as blue, and flaxen hair, who hadn't ever worked a minute and hadn't ever thought they would. Because of this, he was apologetic when she labored beside him, which made her think only that he was kind. She realized, after all, that the milk she drank and the cheese she ate came from their cows, and that the cows ate the hay that she cut and carried. Thus the work appeared to her to be justified not only by custom but by economics.

Still, he was moved and proud to see her sitting in a corner of the porch, recovering from the heat, with streaks of salt on her sunburned face. Although she had been through storms, blizzards, and dark days, and although she knew loneliness, cold, and hunger, she had never encountered deception, malice, or greed, and was sure that if she did she could easily defeat them. Her confidence showed in her pure and open expression.

"Do you still think about descending to the plain to look for your mother and father?" he asked, because, especially now, he did not want her to leave.

"Yes," she answered.

"All right," he said. "Next year, at the beginning of summer,

I'll send you down with Anna."

"Who will help with the harvest?" she asked.

"I can do it myself. Anna will take you. Besides, by harvest time you might even be back."

"Why don't *you* take me? Why do I have to go with Anna? I don't want to go with her. Her eyes refuse to look at anything but the end of her broom."

"Don't say that about Anna. It's not kind. Anyway, I can't go down there."

"Why not?"

"I don't want to."

"Don't want to, or can't?"

"Both. As you get older," he said, "they tend to merge. You tire of some things, and most of all of repeating them — either in action or in thought. I would grow impossibly tired of reliving my life there. Here, I don't have to replot all my battles."

"But you did great things," she insisted. "You knew the emperor. Anna told me you did."

"Anna should never have spoken about that."

"Isn't it true?"

"Yes, I knew the emperor. But he is the emperor no longer,

and though the people surrounding him thought they shared in his glory, they woke up to find that they had been eating ashes. My life was a failure, until I came here and unsaddled myself of ambition."

"How old were you then?"

"Almost sixty."

She looked at him blankly, unable to imagine the passing of sixty years.

"Perhaps you should know a little of what occurred in my life before you were born," he said, "now that you want to go down there, where things are so different."

As he began to speak she folded her knees up against her chest and rested her chin on them in perfect comfort, with the flexibility of those under ten. The crickets were singing in the afternoon heat, and the background they provided for his story was like a golden brocade.

"I'll tell you how I came to know the emperor, but you must not ever repeat it. This is not to protect me, but to protect you. I am far from reprisal, and his reign is long over.

"All my life, I followed my own nose, and was willing to be poor and scorned, since my father brought me up to believe that agreement between more than two people, no matter how sensible or just, quickly becomes a dangerous form of illusion and is soon bound up with pride and power-seeking. I gave free rein to my inclinations — a great luxury, I admit — in books and articles that I wrote, and was able to do so because I ignored the punishments meted out to those who do not conform. I was always ready to embark upon physical labor — as I have done — having known since my childhood the delight of a good day's work in the fields."

"But it's so hard," the little girl said, and she spoke from experience.

"Of course it's hard, but the harder you work, the better you feel — provided that you have some land, as we do, and can grow a good crop."

She nodded gravely.

"When you work in the sun, in your own field, there are no illusions that destroy precious time, no opinions, no intrigues — only infallible natural laws, and they never betray you . . ."

"And when you're sick?"

"That is no betrayal. God and nature promise mortality, and sickness is the rehearsal." He stopped himself short. Though she was attentive, she was uncomprehending, as perhaps she should have been at her age. So he continued.

"I had a difficult career as those things go. I managed in just a few years to alienate almost everyone in the capital, and yet I turned to no one for aid or protection. As you know, I found the very fact of people in comfortable agreement objectionable. It actually caused me to have the physical feeling that African termites were crawling all over my body, which is the same feeling I get when I have to wear formal dress.

"The older I got, the poorer I became, until I had to live in a small part of the attic of a barn on a turkey farm at the edge of the city. The roof was so low that I could only stand up in the center of the floor, and I was always smashing my face into beams."

"That's terrible!"

"I managed. I had learned to look far beyond oblivion, and I was not disappointed in what I saw."

"I mean about the beams."

"Oh. Just a few bruises, nothing serious. Anyway, one rainy night, as I was trying to work by the light of a turkey-fat lamp — I could hardly see: turkeys are not known for the brilliance of their fat — I heard horses gallop up to the barn. It sounded like a patrol of dragoons.

"I thought it was the tax authorities, come to count the turkeys. They did that, you know, even in the middle of the night. Then they would come into my garret to measure my furniture and weigh my ink bottles. Once, they counted the feathers in my pillow and taxed me on the excess over five hundred, plus interest and penalties for every night that I didn't sleep with an Indonesian dictionary balanced on my chest. 'Why?' I asked. 'You must assume,' they told me, 'that we require everything of you, and that you are free to do only what we specifically exempt. We have exempted all other parts of the body and all other materials from the night-balance requirement. Also, it is your right to substitute for the Indonesian dictionary any five consecutive journals of the Brazilian Anti-Stuttering League. Mind you, if you do so, you must file the appropriate forms as specified in our bulletins, and you are responsible for keeping the forms updated as their format changes.'

"But that night the sound of boots did not stop in the barn, for turkey counting. Up the stairs it came. There was a knock at my door, a polite knock, almost a French knock. I answered it. A colonel and his subalterns snapped to attention on the landing. Their lantern blinded me. 'What do you want?' I asked in the tiny voice that exists for tax collectors.

" 'The emperor requests that he honor you by allowing you to meet him,' they said.

" 'Me?'

" 'Are you the genius who recently proposed a balloon bridge over the Danube?'

" 'Yes.'

" 'Then you're it.'

" 'What emperor?'

" 'There is only one, sir.'

"When they saw that I was frozen in disbelief and could not have moved by myself, they picked me up by the arms. On our way down the stairs I asked if I should not change into better clothes.

" 'Do you have any?' they asked.

" 'No,' I said, shaking my head.

"We galloped through the capital, rattling windows in coffee houses and putting out street lamps with the sweep of cool air that followed our massive Damavand horses. I had always walked across the city. Now I flew. I wondered what I might have done to offend the emperor — did he detest balloon bridges? — and in so wondering, my sense of strength returned. I would not fear him if he had decided to punish me. I would not fawn on him or try to curry favor if he had chosen to reward me. I would ignore the material trappings that men of high station use to hypnotize those over whom they wield power. In short, I decided to remember where we both stood in the eyes of God, and to be myself rather than some special persona invented to please or defy him.

"At the palace, they took me through ten thousand heavily gilded rooms and corridors lit by fireplaces as big as the gates of a brewery, and candelabra that looked like flaming trees. Orchestras sounded in several directions. I peered out the window of one long hall and saw in a ballroom across a courtyard at least a thousand men and women dancing quadrilles."

"What are quadrilles?"

"I don't know. Whenever I see a large number of people

dancing, I assume they are dancing quadrilles.

"Imagine the volume of calculation going on in the minds of those privileged folk as they danced. It must have shamed the counting houses of Bessarabia. And they all were scheming to gain favor in the eyes of those whose eyes had looked upon the emperor himself. Meanwhile, I, in my pantaloons with holes in the knees, was being walked past them right to the man of whom they dreamed. And how did I get myself in such an envied position? I didn't do anything. I merely said what I took to be the truth, with no calculation whatsoever. And I had never had the desire to be in the emperor's good graces, since a man of my profession, unless he has betrayed what has brought him to it in the first place, has no need of favors.

"Now, you would think that the emperor would be some sort of giant in very fancy clothes, sitting on a throne in a high tower somewhere in his labyrinthine palace, surrounded by beautiful young women in coquettish fluster and officers throwing out their chests like combat pigeons. Not at all. They brought me to a white-bearded bald old fellow who was lying on a worn Turkoman carpet in front of a half-dead fire. He had a book beside him, a catalogue of his railroad bridges, and he held a pen

between his toes. He used his magnificent, sleepy, burgundy-and-gold-colored hunting dogs — dozens of them, Anatoles, Purgamanians, Zywynies, Bosteroles, and Voolenhausers — as pillows and rugs. Even if he rested his elbow on one's head, it only wrinkled up its eyes and continued its dream of fetching birds from the reeds. It was an odd and tranquil scene. And you could hear strains of a waltz coming from deep within the palace.

" 'Are you the emperor?' I asked, because at first I thought he might be a dog-handler or a groom.

"This seemed to amuse him. It was he: I recognized him from postage stamps.

" 'No wonder you're the emperor,' I said. 'You can write with your foot.'

" 'Not really. I just keep my pen there sometimes,' he answered. 'But wait, maybe I can. What an excellent way to send orders to my foot soldiers. Call for a tablet.'

" 'How?'

" 'Just call.'

" 'Just say *tablet*?'

" 'Yes, my voice is tired.'

" 'I'm not used to giving orders.'

" 'I am. Do it.'

" 'Tablet!' I screamed. The door flew open so quickly that I jumped back in surprise, and a liveried servant appeared with a vellum tablet. While I held it, the emperor tried to write with the pen held in his toes. He didn't do very well. Then he had me try it. I didn't do very well either. Now I breathed a little easier, because I knew we had something in common.

" 'Venison pâté and blackberry juice!' he shouted. The door popped open, and they appeared. We began to eat and drink.

"I could no longer ignore his costume. 'Are those pajamas?' I asked.

" 'Of course not! This is military underwear! Today I inspected a regiment of my hussars.'

" 'In underwear?'

" 'Yes, in underwear, with a uniform over it.' He pointed to a uniform hanging on a wooden peg near the fire, and threw a piece of wood into the dying flames.

"Noting the heavy pistol on the belt of his tunic, I asked, 'Do you need a license to carry that?'

" 'Me?'

" 'Yes.'

" 'I don't think so. I think, as far as I know, that *personally* I can do anything I want.'

" 'Can you cross the street against traffic?'

" 'When I'm around, there isn't any. They block off all the roads.'

" 'That means you've never seen vehicular congestion.'

" 'Only from a distance,' he said, and then, with some concern that I might think he had led a protected life (as if he hadn't), he added, 'I've seen lots of troops, though, and lots of birds flying around. Pheasants, you know, when flushed in great numbers, tend to bump and collide. What would you call that?'

" 'I would have great difficulty finding a name for it.'

"And then, as if to change the subject, he said, 'I find this venison pâté a trifle too rich. It appears to be seventy percent truffles, and it should be fifty percent. We must have had a rotation in the corps of pâté chefs.'

" 'I think it's magnificent,' I said. 'Anyway, it's better than turkey feet.'

" 'To me,' he said with a sigh, 'it's like potatoes. I have it all the time. I say it and it appears. It's boring, but how can the populace live without it?'

" 'They've never had it, that's how.'

"After a silence, he asked, 'Have you ever played *le grand choisule?*'

"I shook my head. *Le grand choisule* was the secret imperial card game. He taught me the suits, jests, combos, and fouls, and we played until four o'clock in the morning. Then he screamed 'Cushion!' and some carefully dressed servants rushed in to station a satin-covered down pillow between his head and a dog. As he fell asleep, I was ushered out.

"For the next year and a half, I went to see him at least twice a week. We kept it secret; no one ever knew."

"Why?" the little girl asked. "Weren't you proud to see the emperor?"

"I was neither proud nor ashamed. That's not the point. I hadn't realized to what extent the emperor was surrounded by counselors and high-level sycophants who measured their lives by how much they could influence his decisions or control his schedule. These people, especially one who was called Von Rothbart, were entirely capable of ordering my assassination merely to assure their position at court. Von Rothbart himself would have been capable of ordering my assassination if he had known that I was getting good at *le grand choisule*. He had once had a waiter decapitated because there were no peppercorns in the pepper grinder.

"Because all the power of the state was concentrated in the person of the emperor, even the littlest things — whom he glanced at during dessert, whether he yawned when he spoke to this or that noble, his sudden affection for the color blue — had profound and exaggerated consequences. If his advisers or the nobility had known that I had been advising him, I wouldn't have lasted very long."

"You advised him?"

"Certainly. We soon tired of playing cards and talking about pheasants. The emperor knew a thousand things about pheasants. But what then? The conversation quickly turned to other topics — semantics, etymology, agriculture, military strategy, aesthetics, diplomacy, and of course politics — with which I had been familiar all my adult life, devoting myself to them with no thought of gain. He had summoned me in the first place because he had read my articles, especially the one about building a bicycle path across the empire, and he wanted to talk.

"Talk we did, for eighteen months. I witnessed the implementation of some of my ideas — hot-chocolate stations on the road to Innsbruck, various types of land reform, free haircuts for varlets — but not many."

"Why not many?" the child asked. "He was the emperor, and could do anything he wanted."

"*Personally.* In matters of *state*, he was much constrained, not least by Von Rothbart, who was almost a shadow emperor. Von Rothbart controlled several divisions and key garrisons of the army, he had his hand deep in the treasury, and he was the director of the secret police. Everyone in the empire was afraid of him. Even his appearance was terrifying. He was taller than any man I have ever seen. He wore black capes and tricornered hats, and he often appeared in domino, which is a mask and hood."

"Why would he want to do that?"

"To frighten people. To build his power, he ruined many a life and took not a few others."

The child seemed not to understand the simple sentence the old man had just uttered.

"You cannot understand," he said, "that to advance his position and aggrandize himself, a man might harm others — and not merely those with whom he was in competition, but innocents."

"What innocents?" she asked.

At this, the old man turned and looked beyond the lines of golden sheaves spread across the fields. He put his hands up to shield his eyes from the bright sunlight.

"What innocents?" she insisted.

"Must you know?"

Though she gave no answer, the answer was clear in the quality of her silence.

"Yes, you must know," he said, and turned back to her, his face flushed in the strong light. "I well understand that you must know, and I will tell you.

"Just to the east of the capital, over the twin channels of the Danube, is a great lake, which you have never seen. It is wide enough that were you to stand on one bank you would not be able to make out a white horse standing on the other, and it is so long that the fastest inland packet takes ten days to go from one end to the other. It bends gently now and then, running flat and smooth below mountains like ours, their white ice reflecting in its deep waters.

"After ten days on the boat, you alight amid the mountains, where a long valley stretches farther still to the east. This is the valley of the Damavand. Three weeks of hard riding on the valley floor will bring you to the easternmost parts of the empire. There, on high plains bereft of forests and lakes, lives a nation of incomparable horsemen. They, the Damavand, are wedded to their horses and appear to grow out of their saddles. Sometimes you see one of them reading a newspaper while standing on the back of his horse as it runs at full speed and takes high walls or hedgerows.

"Partly because of their inordinate fascination with horses and horsemanship, their province is not economically well developed. But, needless to say, they mount the best cavalry the world has ever seen, and it is they who defend the eastern borders of the empire from the Golden Horde. They need not be but they are intensely loyal, and they have always been allowed to run their own affairs, both from gratitude and from necessity. For you cannot tame them; they are horsemen who are born with a blue horizon in their eyes, and no matter how fast they gallop, that horizon recedes.

"The Damavand princes traced their ancestry to the remark-

able men who watched from the ground as the Golden Horde conquered their land and burned their dwellings, and who then bravely and ingeniously took to horseback themselves, surprising their conquerors from the rear and the flank, trapping them against the wall of the mountains, and annihilating them. What did it take for sedentary farmers to mount and suddenly become ravishing cavalry? It took a miracle, and as their joy at exceeding their own expectations spread from troop to troop, it made even the captured nomadic horses happy to go against their former masters.

"Unlike western princes, the Damavand did not live in brittle palaces but in brightly colored tents. They went freely among their subjects and were hard riders. Their wealth was in their horses, their herds, and the great monasteries they endowed. All the emperors, from the very beginning, had treated them with respect. The eastern province had always been fertile, content, and marvelously strong.

"Von Rothbart, however, could not resist making inroads to the east. Unbeknownst to the emperor, he sent brigades of fusiliers and garrisoned them on the plains, he increased taxes little by little, and he drafted Damavand cavalry to serve in places as remote and inhospitable to them as the West Glaciers and the Baltic herring flats.

"At first the Damavand made no protest, as there was much they would tolerate in their loyalty to the empire. But as the pressures grew, Prince Esterhazy, their sovereign, guessed that they might be suffering without the emperor's consent. He decided to go to the capital and petition the emperor directly, and to take with him his wife — who was tall, beautiful, and blonde like her Kazakh forebears — and their daughter, the infant Princess Odette.

"The Damavand princes had always been taught self-reliance and frugality. Because of this, and because he wanted to make good time, Prince Esterhazy dispensed with his retainers and set out for the capital. The infant princess was strapped tightly to her mother's back as her mother and father galloped west on two horses, one white and one gray.

"After they had been on the road for several days and had come to the steep cliffs that form the west wall of the province, they were accosted by a group of bandits in a defile where the road narrows to almost nothing. The bandits stood by their horses and blocked the path, expecting the prince and his wife to wheel and run. A slide of heavy rocks and tree trunks had been readied to trap them in retreat.

"But the prince spurred his horse forward, his wife followed suit, and their heavy mounts rammed the bandits' mountain ponies, sending three of them, and their masters, into a rushing river far below, from which they were never to emerge. As his wife and child pulled ahead, the prince held back, and turned in the saddle.

"While his horse was cantering smoothly along the road, he calmly removed from his quiver a short and powerful Mongol bow. The bandits had firearms, and as they gained on him they fired wildly. But only when they were within range did he draw the bow and loose his first shot. An arrow of lignum vitae and steel penetrated the breast of one of the bandits with the sound of a cleaver splitting an apple, and neatly removed him from the saddle. This action was so smooth and quick that the other bandits hadn't time to know it for what it was, and they still thought the prince had his back to them. They continued on. When they fired, he did not flinch, for flinching would have done him no good. Instead, he drew his bow for a second time. The bow's short length hardly showed, but the second arrow, heavy and straight, flew through the air and felled one of the four remaining bandits as if he had collided with an oak limb hanging over the road. One second he was on his horse, and less than a second later he wasn't. Suddenly the others brought their horses to a halt.

"The farther west Prince Esterhazy, his wife, and the child sailed on the lake steamer, the more foreign and outlandish they seemed in their seminomadic costume. As horsemen and foresters debarked at easterly ports, they took with them the ways of the Damavand and were replaced by farmers who lived in chalets in well-ordered fields, and then by merchants and professionals returning from vacation cottages with white fences, beds of geraniums, and stone terraces abutting the water. City dwellers in carefully tailored suits, patent boots, and steel-rimmed spectacles stared at the prince as if he had put on his clothes that morning solely for the purpose of offending them.

"Two heads taller than any of the onlookers, the prince filled them with awe, apprehension, and contempt, for they had been raised to 'see and be seen,' whereas he and his wife were riders of horses and interpreters of clouds. He didn't notice the stares and comments, some of them quite nasty. This was to prove his undoing. In capital cities you must take account of gossip and fashion as if they were arrows flying at you. The minor cruelties uttered at dinner parties and in cafés are endowed with a power out of all proportion, but the prince from the far province would not have understood the pettiness of the ruling circle even had he been aware of it. After all, in the Damavand the horizon was synonymous with the curve of the earth, and both were always in sight.

"He did not go immediately to see the emperor. After two weeks' travel, he wanted to rest, and he and his wife found accommodation at a modest inn. They spent days walking the boulevards, amazed that horses pulled enormous wheeled boxes in which people read books and newspapers and drank tiny cups of chocolate, coffee, and tea. In the Damavand, tea was served in a glass. In the capital, they drank from nothing larger than thimbles.

"The little princess was delighted by the animals in the zoo. Though she was completely used to horses, she had never seen a rhinoceros or a giraffe, both of which she found infinitely fascinating because she thought they were horses that had failed to measure up.

"Her parents carefully placed her on the diminutive rides in the children's park. At an archery booth, the prince gathered every prize but one, a rubber artichoke, because he did not understand what it was. They even took the baby to the opera. This was unheard of, and elicited rude stares. But what did they care? They had never heard of opera. They liked it, though, for it reminded them of the open plains they knew so well, even though it transpired in a room with a ceiling. This they thought a miracle worthy of further investigation.

"But they paid dearly for these enjoyable days. Von Rothbart's agents were everywhere and could not help but note so outlandish a family. Their reports languished for a week in a pigeonhole at the headquarters of the secret police, but finally made their way through the bureaucracy until a middle-level official recognized them for what they were. Von Rothbart was delighted. He knew the prince had not seen the emperor, for he knew exactly whom the emperor saw (that is, except for me), and he sent a little spy in a black cape with crimson lining — the man looked like a bat — to the inn, deep in a pine grove, where the prince and his family were staying. The spy confirmed the reports.

"Over a period of several days, Von Rothbart sent five bow-men, each disguised as a traveler, to the inn. These 'salesmen' and 'solicitors' took up positions in rooms facing an inner court-yard. There they waited, peering through the cracks in the shutters. One evening at dusk, the prince and his wife, who carried Princess Odette in her arms, returned from the center of the city and began to walk across the courtyard to their rooms.

"As the lead bowman flung open his shutters, the others followed suit. When the prince heard this, he looked up with great apprehension and saw the archers in the windows, their bows drawn. Before he could put his arms around his wife and daughter, the arrows were released, and each found its way with terrible precision.

"The prince himself was struck by three arrows, and his wife was pierced by two others. They fell, and as soon as they hit the flagstones another volley arrived, doubling their wounds, and then, when they were immobile, another, and then, even after they were dead, another, as fast as the bowmen could set and let fly their arrows.

"Though the prince had thrown himself over his wife too late, she had shielded the child. They died not so much in physical pain as with the far greater anguish of not knowing the fate of their daughter. The child herself was too shocked to cry out, and lay crushed beneath her mother, covered with blood, in a state that I, for all the things I have seen, cannot imagine.

"The assassins fled, not for fear of being caught but because even they had to flee from the horror of what they had done. They had been instructed to kill the child too, and when their hail of arrows brought complete silence to the little courtyard, they thought they had, because babies cry. They reported to Von Rothbart that he would not be harried by an avenging heir.

"Despite what Von Rothbart thought, the child was alive and unhurt. As soon as the assassins fled, a scullery maid who had witnessed the murders, with no idea whatsoever of why they had occurred, rushed to lift the baby from underneath her mother and father. The maid left on the instant, with the baby in her arms. She did not stop for a moment, and traveled all night on the forest road and for many days thereafter, never returning to the capital. The infant Princess Odette, whose name and a crown were embroidered on her gown, did not cry that terrible night, or any night thereafter, for all her tears had been taken from her."

"Rumors spread through the capital, and whether by hope or by some lively quality of the truth people said that the child of the murdered couple had been spared and had been taken into the forest.

"Day after day, Von Rothbart sent waves of soldiers to search the countryside. Patrols searched every barn within ten days' travel of the Josefstädterstrasse. They searched the immense forest, its lakes, gorges, and stands of giant trees. They discovered an almost infinite number of compassionate hiding places. Once, the woman and child heard horsemen riding through a meadow. They listened as the grasses rustled and broke and the horses snorted, and they retreated into the shadows of a thick glade of trees. The horsemen passed by.

"To excuse their failure in hunting down the child, the soldiers said that her nurse had turned her into a white swan. This was readily believed in the capital not so much because people thought it was true but because they held out hope for her, and her transformation into so graceful a creature seemed both beautiful and just. Still, Von Rothbart would have kept his soldiers out for months, had not everything been eclipsed by the death of the emperor.

"The emperor was an old man, and yet everyone was shocked when he died, for emperors are supposed to be as imperturbable as the state they embody. He was playing chess with the empress when suddenly he threw his arm across the board, upsetting all the pieces, as if he were reaching for a ledge to stop a fall. Though his last words were reported to have been 'Let whosoever comes after me govern wisely and with self-sacrificing justice,' he said in fact, 'Apologize to my pheasants!' No one knew whether he was remorseful or believed the empress had somehow slighted the inhabitants of his hunting preserves. It didn't make any difference. For him, it was all over.

"In the convulsion that followed, Von Rothbart forgot about Princess Odette. As the spring ice broke up on every lake in the empire, he spent his energies in desperate maneuver, and after months of politicking, bribery, and violence, succeeded in making himself regent for the emperor's newborn son, a royal prince who was the first male child in the kindly emperor's forty years of fathering. Though dozens of the emperor's children were scattered over the continent, some already wise and middle-aged, the heir to the throne was a little cross-eyed baby not much bigger than a bullfrog. Von Rothbart, as he saw it, had eighteen or twenty years to make fast his hold on the empire.

"But the emperor had not been a fool. He knew that Von Rothbart would have twenty years' sway, and would watch the boy's development with deep interest. So, to allay Von Rothbart's suspicions, he chose a tutor with no political allies and no support from any faction. He instructed the tutor to appear publicly to be a bumbling and impotent scholar, ignorant of power politics and obsessed with the arcane debates of cosmology and taxonomy; to teach the prince the fundamentals, with an eye to creating within him not only compassion but courage; to make sure that the prince was secretly tutored in combat; and, finally, to wait until the right moment and then entrust the prince with the task of overturning Von Rothbart or whoever had succeeded him. He added, in a letter setting out the requirements, that the tutor should appear to be fond of drink, for Von Rothbart would be delighted to see the prince's teacher crippled by the ceaseless consumption of alcohol."

"How do you know this?" the girl asked, sweeping back a lock of hair. "How could you possibly know?"

"I was the tutor."

"Ah!" the child exclaimed.

"Ah, indeed! I had to pretend to be an alcoholic, which was difficult for me, since my stomach refuses alcohol in any form. I took lessons from a Hungarian actor, and soon was able to appear perpetually intoxicated. I became so good at this that sometimes I had difficulty getting sober.

"Von Rothbart had never heard of me, and did not know of my association with the emperor. In the half-dozen interviews he commanded, I exhibited a great passion for frogs. When he asked me about politics, I told him about the digestive system of frogs. I offered to tutor him in this infinitely fascinating branch of the sciences, and though he seemed extremely pleased, he politely declined. He seemed delighted also by the fact that I stammered in his presence, laughed weakly for no reason, and contrived never to look him in the eye. These humiliations allowed me twenty years to raise a young man upon whom the hope of the empire could rest.

"You would have liked him, I know, as a boy, and as a young man. I had to make him immediately aware of the sadness and tragedy in the world, for failing that, he would not have been able to develop the latent powers that promised, very quietly, to make him an emperor in his own right. He was a serious child most of the time, somewhat like you. I think I did well by him, though he had to be brought up, unlike most princes, with a broken heart."

"The young prince was nearly an orphan. Of course, he had every material advantage, and he even slept in a gold cradle. But, uninfected with the stupidity of their elders, infants can neither crave nor value things like that. In fact, Princess Odette, raised at the same time with only pine boughs for a roof, was probably better off than he, with his nursery the size of a great railway station."

"What about his mother, the queen?"

"The empress."

"The empress, then."

"She was the daughter of minor nobility in the Tyrol. They were what you find *underneath* the bottom of the barrel. They dressed up their daughter to catch the eye of someone in the capital who could support them, and succeeded beyond their wildest expectations, for when the emperor's first wife died he was so confused that he fastened upon the bottom-of-the-barrel girl as if she were heaven itself. She was beautiful, that I will admit, but her interests were confined to dresses, jewelry, and the flattery of half a hundred attendants. During the time she was with child she was so ashamed of her appearance that she fled to the upper storeys of the palace and was not seen in public. And after the prince was born, she gave him over to a wet nurse and took the court to Bogdelice-by-the-Sea.

"She ordered that he be dressed well, and saw him mainly on ceremonial occasions. The rest was left to the staff. Before the emperor had been in his grave two weeks, she began to have affairs, and do you know with whom she formed the most lasting liaison, merely because he was able to flatter her most falsely and procure for her the rarest jewels?"

"Who?"

"Guess."

"No!"

"Yes. Von Rothbart. I had quite a task. The boy had no father, and, in a sense, no mother. I had to keep him un-damaged by Von Rothbart, make him strong, and prepare him to take by force the empire to which he was heir.

"The saddest and hardest thing was that I could not let him love me like a father, which meant that I could not appear to love him, as I did, like a son. Whenever we approached such a point — if, for example, he was playing and he reached out to embrace me — I had to draw away."

"But why?" the child asked, since he had not raised her that way.

"Perhaps mistakenly, I believed I had to save a great place in his heart for the father he had never known. Taking on Von Rothbart and his allies would be something the prince would have to do for his own blood, to please a father who could never be pleased. Since I myself did not need an empire salvaged, I would not have been sufficient to fill that place.

"I did succeed in bringing up a serious and troubled young man, which was my aim, since wisdom comes not from fair weather but from storms. And by the time he was eighteen, he was competent in half a dozen languages, the classics, mathematics, and military strategy. He had, of course, studied the history of kingdoms and empires.

"From the time he was little, I had taken him out into the

countryside. No one missed him. His mother was too involved with the life of the court to know that we had gone on foot toward Klagenfurt, just the two of us, with me dressed in my pants with holes in the knees, and him in his roughest play clothes. We were on the road for several months of the year, mainly when the weather was good and everyone had gone to the summer palace. Because of this, he understood ordinary people, and was neither gullible nor imperious. He knew he was not to say who he was. It didn't matter; no one would have believed him anyway.

"Once, we camped by a river with boys who were the sons of merchants in Immelstädt and had run away to hunt and climb. For three weeks they were lost in their own society, the prince with them, an equal. They reached the summits of several nearby peaks, they swam in the river and set up a rope off which they flew into a deep pool, and they hunted, although he was profoundly troubled by the killing of helpless animals. It was hard for me to take him back home. He preferred their kind of life to his own. But he had no choice.

"When he was older, I set up a camp in the forest, where we went in the greatest secrecy for military training. I brought

in swordsmen, cavalry riders, and archers from the Damavand, which by that time had already rebelled against the empire. Here were the finest soldiers of their kind, practiced in combat against troops fighting under the name of the prince, risking their lives to train him as best they could.

"Von Rothbart and the empress were under the impression that the prince was physically incapable of wielding anything heavier than a plume. We deliberately kept away from sports. He neither hunted nor rode, and had no fencing master. Do you understand how that looked? Even the dairymaids had fencing masters. They thought the prince had been cut off at the knees, which pleased Von Rothbart immensely. But he wouldn't have been pleased had he seen the prince, tutored intensively from the age of four, with a bow, on a horse, or exercising with a saber. No saber master had his strength or alacrity, no cavalryman could turn as well in the saddle or fight with a sword while hanging under his horse. And with his heavy bow the prince could shoot the pips off apples across the Danube so quickly that you would have thought three archers were at work much closer to the targets.

"Boys in late adolescence, even if they are not royal princes, even if they do not excel in marksmanship and other such things, can get astoundingly smug. And why not? They are in the peak of health. Nature itself makes them want to sing and dance. And, in the main, they do not know grievous loss.

"Had he been just anyone, this kind of natural arrogance would have served to power him through the difficult years of his twenties. But he had extraordinary responsibilities. I had to season him, and did so by making him face before he had to the great and insoluble questions that come to us in the normal course of a lifetime, both in suffering and in understanding.

"I confronted him by example (for we had the resources to seek such examples, and it was the right time in history) with death and dying — two different things entirely — with the suffering of children, the slaughter of innocents, and those things of similar gravity that perplex and hurt me not less, but more, as I grow old.

"At first, as I had expected, he gave me facile answers. And just as I had had to withdraw when, as a child, he had come to me with open arms, now I took from him his youth and substituted for it only sadness, confusion, and bitterness. I disillusioned him.

"This was just before his coming of age, an occasion that I knew would be dear to the empress, for then she could gorge herself on ceremony and force him to choose a wife who would resemble her. I also knew that with the prince's coming of age Von Rothbart, now quite old, just as fierce, and triply dangerous, would take certain measures even though he thought the young man was effeminate.

"The empress and Von Rothbart wondered why the prince was so melancholy. Though he did all he was supposed to do — he went to the balls and feasts, and he danced — he was melancholy, and he could not hide it."

"When the prince came of age they had a series of damnable parties and pageants which were no good to anyone except bakers, florists, and the poets and composers commissioned to write odes. Before I was transported from my loft on the turkey farm to my quarters in the royal palace, I had been commissioned to write odes for the declining nobility — *Ode on the Birthday of Baron Stumpf, Ode to the Daughter of Principessa*

Tantoweeni, Ode on the Restoration of the Pergola at the Country Seat of the Duchess of Tookisheim. I called them odes, all right. I always said 'Ode damn' when I had to write one. You break your head for two weeks, and they pay you enough to take a spider to lunch."

The little girl was delighted by this professional complaint, for it suggested that the world was full indeed if the farmer she had known for as long as she could remember could have led at one time so different a life. "What about your quarters in the palace?" she asked. "Were they as big as our house, or bigger?" She was referring to a good cedar cabin, with inimitable views, that was big enough only for the two of them and Anna, with whom she did not want to go down to the plain.

"Really!" he answered. "We are talking about the greatest palace that has ever been built. When I lived in it, it had some seventeen thousand five hundred rooms, a few of which could comfortably hold ten thousand people as they walked around dressed in absurd balloon-like clothing. Eight cavernous halls were used just for storing the keys to the scores of thousands of doors. I knew an old fellow whose title was Cartographer of the Palace and whose job was to teach palace geography to teachers

who would then teach servants, mechanics, and the royal family itself.

"To get a message from one part of the palace to another, you put it in a small box and sent it by dumbwaiter to express riders on the roof. They had a system of roads and bridges up there that took four days to cover. Inside, running unseen through the entire structure, were vast service corridors through which traveled horse-drawn wagons laden with firewood, candles, ashes, linens, and flowers.

"The river Von Blimpen diverted into the northern end of the palace and exited in the south. You could row a boat down the tunnel, near the top floor, from which water was drawn into boilers, tubs, fountains, pools, and sinks.

"There were indoor hunting preserves, huge tanks for staging mock naval battles, hospitals for hunting birds, grouse-plucking galleries, and pheasant egg incubators. Once, I was surprised to stumble upon a training academy for truffle-sniffing pigs. Each pig had a groom and two handlers, and lived in a big bedroom with *trompe l'oeil* depictions of an oak forest. The classrooms and auditoriums of this academy were tucked into the asparagus storage section of the green spring vegetable kitchens.

"My quarters were perfectly compatible with all this. I had ten bedrooms. What could I do with ten bedrooms? I had twenty bathrooms. One of the bathrooms had its own bathroom, and one had a bathtub so big that it had been used to keep a blue whale that had been trucked from Gibraltar in a giant brine wagon. The library was another thing — five million volumes and two hundred librarians. I had dozens of aides: chefs, tailors, footmen, boatmen, huntsmen, puntsmen, and even acrobats, whom I used to illustrate to the prince the laws of gravity and motion.

"Needless to say, this was too rich an atmosphere for real study, and I used to take him out into the garden, where we would sit on a step and do lessons. In winter we would set up a lamp and work at a heavy wooden table in the idled strawberry kitchens.

"I quickly understood why the emperor had lived in a small room with a worn Turkoman carpet. One of the grandeurs of human beings is that they tire of grandeur. Yes, I like quail eggs on occasion. But eight hundred pounds a day?

"Anyway, when the prince came of age they had an exhausting series of expensive parties. I detest parties. Because of the action on all sides, you must be alert and are constantly distracted. Everything is broken up into the smallest and most inconsequential bits, for which the only integrative antidote is alcohol, of which I, for medical reasons, cannot partake. And besides, I do not want to hear about the wonderful swimming party at the Duchess of Tookisheim's river palace, thank you very much. And I do not want to talk to the Marquis of Steubenplotz about how he lost his teeth on grapeshot in the ostriches he killed, while all the time he is looking across the room for a glimpse of the empress, as if he were a railroad signalman peering into a tunnel from which he feared might explode the express to Saarbrücken. These affairs were insufferable, and at every odd one I was obliged to play drunk. I sacrificed for my prince, and he knew it.

"At the last of these before the great extravaganza at which he was to choose a wife, he was doing his best to be charming. You see, he was not the smooth youth that he was supposed to have been. He had great difficulty being polite to people whom he really wanted to pick up and swing over his head. When he was not smiling, his eyes were too deep and his face too weathered and wise to be the face of an ineffectual boy. I believe this unsettled Von Rothbart, who didn't know what to make of it.

"The empress appeared, and the prince went through the motions of respect, though he hardly knew her. When he and I looked at her we always saw Von Rothbart's tricornered hat bobbing behind her head, like a bumblebee. Ostensibly she had come to inform the prince that at the next ball he would be surveying princesses, to choose one for eternity, or at least that small part of it in which we imagine that we know what transpires. In this she took great pleasure and he none at all. Everyone knew the schedule. She just wanted to drive it in.

"When she left, the prince could not conceal his unhappiness. To cheer him up, one of the courtiers proposed that we all go hunting. As the sun was due to rise in an hour, this suggestion was enthusiastically received, because the animals would be careless and dreamlike at dawn, and the hunters would have an easy time shooting them. The prince did not want to waste his time, but they virtually carried him away.

"I was old enough to escape such obligations, and I did not go, but much later, upon his return, my pupil told me a wonderful story with which, although he did not realize it, I was already partially familiar.

"Half the joy of hunting is to ride with a hundred horsemen, weapons at your side, thundering over wooden bridges over thundering streams. I do not know the other half. The hunt is only an excuse to form an army and exercise at war, and is one of those things treasured mainly in remembrance. The violent motion of a war horse on the run becomes in immediate recollection as smooth as a waltz. How the peaks and valleys of the gallop are beaten into silky waves I do not know, except that memory is the greatest poet.

"If the prince rode at the head of his courtiers and soldiers on such an expedition, he had to discipline himself and his mount not to pull ahead, because he was supposed to be scared of horses. No one dared pass him until he waved them on, and he did wave them on, quite early. As they overtook him, all agreed to go right when they reached the fork in the forest road, for to the right were the glades in which ran fierce wild boar, and the soldiers were not as fond of hunting birds as they were of mortal combat with the squat berry-eating pigs that could bite off a man's leg as if it were a celery stalk.

"When the prince, now alone, reached the fork in the road, he went left. Veering from the main body enabled him to ride as fast as he wanted to ride, to appear — according to my instructions — fearful of the clash with the boar, to find truly deserted and forgotten country, and merely to watch the birds and deer that, in the company of others, he would have been expected to kill.

"He had no desire to kill animals. This was owing not so much to compassion as to respect, for not even memory can conspire to make a smoother line than the track of a bird wheeling silently in the sunshine over blue water. And when deer step gingerly in the heather, their precision of motion is art, and that is not to mention the perfect rocketry of their escapes. Were they to go faster, the result would not be so pleasing, and were they to go slower, they would not appear to be nobly disciplining themselves against flight.

"The prince rode hard for several hours. When he dismounted, he had come to the shore of a vast lake teeming with emerald-and-gray ducks, white swans, and checkered loons. He rested his horse and began to climb a granite cliff that rose straight from the lake. Up he went, past sinewy pines in the cracks, and steplike ledges as smooth and narrow as balcony rails, hanging perilously over the sparkling water, until he reached the top — a dry, lichen-covered floor that seemed to overlook the whole world. A ridge led south to uncharted mountains, but though he looked for a long while at their high and alluring meadows, he turned finally to the lake.

"The lake was a blue jewel that had been broken by the sunlight into infinitely sequined brass. He had to shield his eyes because its surface had become a hundred million little flares. Though the light hurt him, he could not turn away from what he saw. Thousands of cloud-white swans were rising on a column of blue air. They made a rotating pillar that stood on the fire of the lake, and, hardly moving their wide wings, they ascended the morning air in a gorgeous spiral at the top of which was nothing less than the sun itself.

"Whether the prince looked up or down, he was assaulted by light too bright to withstand. And yet the movement of the swans, perfectly orchestrated, held him fast until he could no longer bear the pain, and he collapsed onto the warm rock. The sun beat down upon him, and as it climbed higher in the sky, everything became a waltz of red and amber in swirling currents of white light and bright silver flashes.

"By dusk, he was burning like fire, but the evening was cool. First came the pale blue and then a black sky, and then moonlight, and mists that rose in unpredictable vales at the lake's edge. He did not know if he were awake or dreaming, but when he opened his eyes and looked down upon the lake, it seemed not so distant. It was as though the water had risen, or he could see magically far.

"As if to echo in their motion the roundness of the moon that bathed them in silver light, the swans were dancing in a ring. Their dance was the perfect union of delirium and control, of purity and abandon, of nature and civilization. How did they put together so gentle a thing with so much power, so powerful a thing with so much grace? It was almost an eastern rite, and yet, they were swans, and yet . . .

"Then he could not believe his eyes, and though he insisted to himself that he was dreaming, the dream was so beautiful that he believed it more than what was real. The swans had become women, and the women had then become swans, until he could not separate them or distinguish between their forms.

"He blinked on purpose. He cleared his throat. What were they that in their silence were so eloquent and in their fragility so strong? He knew that dreams and delirium, like fire, can give warmth and heat but cannot finally be grasped. But he knew as

well that what he saw before him was so beautiful that it had to be substantial, for imagination could not have been so fine. And though he had been brought beyond his understanding, he refused not to credit his dream with all the depth of the world.

"Then he awakened. He was not in the palace, but still in the forest, though he could tell by the cry of the loons that he was no longer on the ledge. He was inside a little hut. He could hardly see. The only light came from a mass of coals in a small mountain stove. The bed was made of cedar, the blankets homespun.

" 'Where is my horse?' he asked a beautiful young woman who was standing near the door.

" 'Outside,' she said.

"As the days passed and the prince recovered, he watched her from his bed. At first he was taken with her physical beauty, and then with her grace. But he knew that he loved her only after he watched her hands as she sewed, and her eyes following her hands. Only when she concentrated on a task outside herself did he apprehend her real beauty, and when he did, he knew real love for the first time.

"You know who she was, though she herself did not, except

for her name, and neither, therefore, could he. She was Odette, and she was the one who, in his dream, had led the swan-maidens in their dance. For this he had a simple explanation. He had seen her when she brought him in, which is why he knew her face, and since the last thing he had remembered had been the swans, he had merely combined the two images. It all made sense — but for the fact that she hadn't brought him in; her companion had.

"When he returned to the city, he told me very little about his stay with her. 'Where have you been?' I asked.

" 'By the shore of a lake, with a woman,' was all he would say.

" 'Who?'

"He shrugged his shoulders.

" 'A milkmaid? Another milkmaid?'

" 'No.'

" 'Who, then?'

"He looked at me blankly.

" 'At least,' I said, 'tell me what she looked like.'

" 'I can't,' he answered. 'You yourself told me that only a painter can describe a face, and then not even he. Faces, you said, are magical. They have not ten features, or twenty, or even two hundred, but thousands, millions, and no deliberate way exists of assessing them.'

" 'But they are appraised easily and immediately in one's heart. I told you that, too.'

" 'Yes, you did.'

" 'And what appraisal did your heart give?'

" 'It told me, from the very first, and then, as each day passed, it told me more and more, that I love her.'

" 'She is a commoner?' I asked. Of course I had nothing against commoners, being one myself, but when a prince falls in love with a commoner, many problems arise.

" 'I don't know,' he said.

Because the prince had been gone for several weeks, all ceremonies had been postponed. Von Rothbart was convinced that the prince was raising an army against him. The foreign princesses at court waited nervously, and they ate so much that they could hardly fit into their fancy dresses.

"When the prince returned, his mother was so enraged that to calm her he told her where he had been. I would have stopped him. But perhaps Von Rothbart would have found him out anyway, either from the love in the prince's eyes, or because he might have been able to recognize the signs of grievance transforming into justice.

"For the second time, Von Rothbart's troops took to the roads in search of Odette. But after his initial indiscretion the prince was quick enough to sense that he had made a mistake, and quick enough still to insist that he had turned on the forest road in the track of the soldiers and courtiers, and, like them, gone off to the right."

"When the prince returned to Odette," the child asked, "did they follow him? I so hope they did not!"

"Things are far more complicated than that," the old man asserted.

"How do you mean?"

"The prince did not go to Odette."

"But he loved her."

"He did. He had come to love her immediately, and she him, which is understandable in view of the circumstances."

"Then why didn't he go to her?"

"He was just old enough to be held by webs of obligation and doubt."

"Webs?"

"For want of a better word."

"I know of no such webs," she said derisively.

"I realize that," the old man answered. "But I do not know how to convey to you how the spirit of a child gradually becomes caged."

She was indignant.

"Don't be upset," he counseled. "One of the great tests in life is to escape that cage while not destroying it. Remaining within it is not inevitable. But you needn't concern yourself with this yet — you're not even ten years old."

He resumed his narrative. "The world of the court and the embassies is more intriguing than you can imagine. Its pleasures sparkle no less for being based entirely on power and privilege, and though they are corrupt, they are hard to refuse. How can I explain them to you?

"On a very superficial level, let us assume that man lives in two worlds: one of God and nature, and the other of his own making. To live entirely in the first and to be satisfied therein is perfectly adequate. Indeed, it is a kind of paradise, which the animals know better than anyone, and without resort to it in some fashion man is nothing more than a machine of his own design. But whereas to live entirely in the world of man is intolerable, to live entirely without it is in some senses equally so. It must be fun to be a squirrel, but think of music, and mathematics, and chocolate cake! The world of man may be imperfection built upon imperfection, but that is what makes it so beguiling — all the accidents and missteps. By the way, do you know why people laugh and animals don't?"

"No," she said, trying to remember if she had ever seen an animal laugh.

"Because people live in a crooked and imperfect place, full of inconsistencies and contradictions. Animals don't laugh because they don't need to: nature is perfect. We have to laugh when we look upon what we have made and what has come of our finely calculated ambitions. Laughter saves us by reconciling our pride to what we really are. Animals — except for cats — have no such need.

"Sometimes, up here where time passes smoothly and slowly, where my own heart, though long broken, is somehow always full, I miss the world below.

"Well, the world of the embassies was self-delighting. Every detail was meant to provide a feeling of walking on air. The women, if not beautiful, contrived to be stunning in appearance, and the artifice they employed had undeniable effect. Powders, perfumes, lotions, dyes, jewels, girdles, pads, and richly colored clothing in combination with a trained bearing can work miracles. For those who were comely to start, the result was breathtaking.

"The food in this world, and I am no lover of any but simple food, had a certain magic. I can't explain it, but the finest food, expertly prepared and served, heightened every word of conversation spoken over it. I cannot comment on the wine, never having been able to drink it. I have mentioned the palace itself. Its fires, flowers, and crystal in great profusion on vast indoor plains of marble and parquet had their own lively effect.

"But none of these things compared with the music. The music was a formula for the most admirable and virtuous intoxication. How they did it — all those musicians, composers, and gypsies — is beyond my understanding, but their music lifted you off the floor and held you effortlessly suspended, lighter than air. For my generation and for those immediately preceding and following, it was the closest approximation we could imagine to the flawless and joyful speech of God.

"The prince was held in place not merely by webs of obligation but by his desire for the world of the court and the embassies, for they had a certain shining, not unlike the sunlit glitter of the lake."

"The princesses assembled in the greatest hall of the palace, the one in which the Duke of Tookisheim used to fly his glider. The prince could just as easily have met them one by one in a small room in one of his apartments, or taken a quiet walk with them in one of the many gardens. That's how I would have done it. Or, assuming it had to be a collective endeavor, I would have had them all working with the prince in stacking firewood or baking a nut log. The best way to know someone is by watching him work or struggle, for then he forgets himself and his qualities either shine through or stay dark.

"But no, the procedure was determined by the empress and Von Rothbart. That meant forty thousand pounds of petits fours and thirty thousand magnums of champagne. All the energies of the empire, of herdsmen in the east, fishermen in the north, foresters in the west, and farmers in the south, the accumulated production of the factories and ateliers, the duty of the soldiers, and the genius of the architects and composers, were distilled into a tiny golden droplet. But it was entrancing. You didn't have to approve of it to admit that it was entrancing.

"Thousands and thousands of overdressed people packed the glider hall. So much perfume was in the air that the palace bees, imprisoned in a far wing, broke loose from their confinements and came through the ventilation system to crisscross ecstatically above the dancers, reflecting the bright gas lamps as if they were golden confetti.

"From the gilded bases of these lamps emerged flames as tall as grenadiers, undulating with the music as if they too were dancing. The orchestra was so tremendous that it overflowed the galleries, and so that he could be seen by all his musicians, little Maestro Nahaag, the conductor, had to stand in a lighted crystal booth suspended from the ceiling by chains. Because the empress thought chains were unsightly, she had had them encrusted with pearls. The waiters looked like generals, and the generals were as colorful as Easter eggs: they were plastered so heavily with medals, tassels, and braid that all you could see of them were two little eyes peeping from a breastwork of lapels, like chipmunks in a stone wall. From within their tunics came brave and muffled descriptions of ancient battles.

"The young prince sat on his father's throne, uncomfortably buttoned up in a red jacket with too much gold braid. Nonetheless, he leaned quite comfortably toward the five princesses. They did look beautiful. And that is not only because they had taken four days to dress, but because they *were* beautiful — except for one, who, although quite homely, was the most charming of the lot.

"After they were presented to him, he danced with them one by one, and as they danced they spoke. Because I noticed their powerful effect, I called him over and told him that Odette was also a princess, though she did not know her origins, and that, unlike her competitors, she was in a state of undiscovered grace.

"But one princess after another courted him, Von Rothbart pressed champagne upon him, and the music made him giddy, as did being compacted in the clouds of perfumed silk that surrounded his dancing partners. Propelled by the magic of her czardas, the Hungarian seemed to be invading his heart, which is not to say that the Russian, the Circassian, the Pole, and the girl from Naples, with their bell-like voices, were not succeeding too.

"Five hours passed, violin strings began to snap, and waiters fainted under trays of caviar and lobster tails. But the celebrants, the cream of the aristocracy, were just getting started. Waltzing around on floors covered with five inches of diamond-hard wax, shoveling down huge loads of highly expensive food, and sitting immobile for many exhausting hours while fat women trilled at them in foreign languages was their profession. People like that get up at seven in the evening, and at a social function the frailest among them, the nonagenarian earls who would not be able to snap a chicken bone to save their lives, or the obese hippocene duchesses who gasp for every breath as if they have swallowed their ropes of pearls, can outlast the greatest athletes who have ever lived.

"I was falling off my feet, pretending to have taken too much champagne, ready to faint from fatigue and discouragement. I had lost all opportunity to influence the prince. He hadn't always listened to me, but now I couldn't even get near him.

"Then the grand waltz began. Ten thousand couples circulated in billowy waves, turning slowly, their forward momentum like that of a wind-driven tide. As beautiful as it was, it still reminded me of bumper cars in the Tivoli. Every now and then I saw the prince floating by, enwrapt in the arms of a magnificent woman.

"At the very peak of the delirium, Von Rothbart jumped up on a marble pedestal, drew a pistol, and fired it in the air. All I could do was watch and regret as a way opened in the hall, and between two ranks of startled aristocrats came the most physically beautiful woman I had ever seen. She was dressed in black, as if to say, 'Judge me by myself alone.' Even now I am unsettled when I think of the perfection and voluptuousness of her features. In her walk across the floor, she seized every eye. The timing of her steps was as rhythmic and even as a dance. She was so graceful that no one would have been surprised had she sailed on the wind and turned as smoothly as a bird.

"Although I didn't know it then, she looked much like Odette, but whereas Odette was open and innocent, she was as

tight as a jewel. Even her name was similar. I winced when Von Rothbart introduced her as Odile.

"In the middle of what had become a hall of pounding hearts, the prince stepped forward, forgetting himself, forgetting all others, forgetting Odette, and held out his arms to take Odile in a dance. When his hand touched hers, it was almost as if we in the hall were ourselves overwhelmed in a real embrace. And when he began to dance with her and their bodies touched, even I, in the depth of defeat, felt pleasure.

"Von Rothbart signaled the conductor, who began a waltz so smooth and hypnotic that it bullied time and banished gravity. A huge sea opened among the dancers. From the sidelines, stunned and delighted guests, and older people who should have been wiser, watched transfixed as the prince and Odile slowly turned across the floor.

"That night he chose her as his bride, and in so doing he chose the world of the court and the embassies over the world of the forest and the lakes."

Hearing this, the child wanted to cry. The old man, however, knew that most stories never really end but, rather, take on a new form, and he continued. "I could think only of Odette," he said. "I hadn't told the prince about her history for fear that he would love her from pity. But now it was too late. Once, I had believed that Von Rothbart's archers had had the last word. Then I had hoped it would not be so. Now, though I felt as keenly for Odette as I might have had I been her father, I had no way to help her. I was deeply moved by the thought of Odette waiting in the forest for the prince, not realizing what he had done, never to see him again. But I didn't know the least of it, for I was not aware that she was soon to bear his child."

"Two years passed. The prince forgot the simple things that once he had loved, and spent his waking hours with Odile, his mother, and Von Rothbart, immersed in the pleasures of the court. In his ceaseless occupation with the flow and control of power and riches and his worship of the cold beauty of Odile, he became a stranger to me, and I was left with my books, instruments, and globes, none of which interested him any longer, and none of which, I confess, interested me. Neither, I might add, did Odile. Apart from her stunning proportions, I could not see what the prince saw in her. She was nearly inanimate, like a rock in a display case, or a portrait that has gone wrong because the painter is a painter more of things than of people.

"But for one incident, about a year and a half after his marriage to Odile, I would have thought that the prince had lost his soul. I was sitting on one of our former tutorial benches, under an overhanging eave in a kitchen courtyard. It was raining heavily, as it must in spring to melt the snow so that summer can blaze across the steppes in green and blue. Watching the rain collide at an angle with a brick wall and then run down it in a tight embrace, I was trying to determine why at a certain volume and force the water bounced off, and why, if neither was sufficient, it didn't. I came to the conclusion that the gross mechanics were directly attributable to the molecular structure of the water, and that the thresholds of adhesion were determined by group particle affinity. I believe I was slightly ahead of my time.

"Anyway, I was intently absorbed, speaking to myself in calculations. When next I looked up, the prince was beside me. 'I didn't see you,' I said.

" 'I know,' he replied. 'You've been muttering numbers in a

kind of song.'

" 'Forgive me,' I said dryly.

" 'Forgiven,' he said, twice as dryly, for he, after all, was a prince. This hurt me, for in truth I did love him like a son.

" 'What were you doing?' he asked.

" 'Calculating the force of impact between a given amount of water and a porous surface, such as brick, necessary for the deflection of the water rather than its adhesion.'

" 'In what units?'

" 'In cubic armands per centipede.'

" 'How can you do that without instruments?'

" 'How can you do it *with* instruments? Estimates — it's all estimates. Just as you fall in love with a voice or a face: all is most powerful precisely in the absence of precision. And since measurement, no matter how exact, is nothing more than an analogy of unfixable quantities, I am, my prince, unafraid to estimate.'

" 'You are unafraid of anything, Tutor, are you not?'

" 'Not so.'

" 'I thought you were fearless. Come, now. You *are* fearless. I believe that you would look into my eyes and tell me that I am corrupt. You would even go against Von Rothbart, wouldn't you?'

" 'Have you become Von Rothbart's spy?' I asked, amazed at his transformation. 'But, yes, certainly I would. That is not what I fear. I am of an age, and I have had a life, whereby I no longer fear what may become of me. But almost as if in compensation, reciprocally, I fear much more and suffer greatly on behalf of others.'

" 'The world in general?' he asked, as if I had been making a political argument.

" 'You know that I am not like that. Love for all is love for none.'

" 'Who, then?'

" 'Those who are pure,' I replied, and it went right to him, for he knew whom I meant. 'Those who suffer. Those who wait.'

"The silence that followed was interrupted as one of the orchestras began to tune in a nearby hall. I have always regarded a first-class orchestra tuning its instruments as a toy shop for the ear. We listened to trumpets, violins, drums, and woodwinds playing their scales, while all the time watching the rain run down the saturated bricks. Then, almost tentatively, the orchestra began to play short but powerful sections from the most beautiful symphonies.

"The wind and rain picked up until the water crossed the threshold of surface tension and molecular adhesion and began to dash off the wall. I turned to the prince, as in the old days, to remark upon this, and when I did I saw that he was looking straight ahead, and that tears were running down his face."

"Soon it was again alpine summer, that cool season unlike any other. Don't ask me how it can contain the freedom and joy of summer simultaneously with the gravity and depth of winter. Ask the mountains."

"I will," the child said, for the mountains were right there, guardians of beauty, immobility, and peace.

"The prince begged me to go on the hunt. I told him that I had no desire to kill anything but Von Rothbart. This was not the kind of joke you made in those times. He laughed anyway, and asked me again. I told him that I was serious, that there was far too much to eat in the palace to justify hunting. I told him that I regretted the idea. I told him half a dozen other things, too. But I went.

"We left early in the morning, half a hundred of us, on the best horses that could be looted from the Damavand. We thundered over the bridges and raced through the forest alleys, intimidating even the pine boughs, which swayed in the breeze as we passed."

"Weren't you frightened?"

"Of what?"

"Of falling off the horse, of the bows and arrows, of the soldiers?"

"Of course not. I knew how to ride a horse. I had been a soldier once, adept with sword and bow."

"You had?" she asked, delighted.

"Yes. Is that so surprising?"

"When?"

"When I was a young man."

"Then you've done everything, Grandfather."

"Not everything," he said, "not yet.

"That day I rode forth with great regret but not without vigor or skill. The prince had long shed the pretense that he was inept, and though he was merely gliding at his ease, the rest of the troop had difficulty keeping up with him.

"These men — the best soldiers of the empire — were so skilled that they loosed arrows on the gallop, left and right, bringing down the animals that the thunder of the Damavand horses' hoofs had flushed from places of refuge. Sometimes the arrows killed the birds and fawns immediately, and sometimes they just wounded them. As we rode, we left scores of stricken animals to die, having reduced creatures of the greatest beauty and grace to nothing. I had seen such things before, of course, and worse.

"The prince took part. I was sure that if he would so wantonly kill, he was lost. But I rode on.

"We exited from the dark forest and its tall, fragrant trees, exploding into the sunlight. Confused and delighted by the brightness, we halted by a lake to water the horses and to rest.

"The fifty Damavand stallions were in an orderly row, their necks bent to drink, their tails swishing, their silken wet flanks glistening in the light. You don't have to hobble Damavand horses near water. They don't run away or spook with water nearby, because they come from a place that's dry.

"Soldiers, huntsmen, and courtiers reclined on a bank. Some slept in the glaring sun. We were all tired, as we had left early in the morning and had been riding hard.

"I too was about to sleep, when I saw the prince sit up with a start. He jumped to his feet, bow in hand, and stepped forward. Almost as if the number had been predetermined, as many swans as there were hunters sailed like a battle fleet around a near point in the lake. Oblivious of the danger, they made right for us.

"Others now awakened and stood, pulling arrows from their quivers and threading their bows. Soon everyone was up, standing silently on the bank, waiting for the procession of swans. When the swans came within shooting distance, I looked sadly at the prince.

"But he had not pulled his bow. He waited, transfixed, until the swans had come too close for sport. Then he turned and commanded that all in our party hold their arrows.

"To see the swans go by and the arrows stayed was for me a great thing. I saw the prince's face change before my eyes. I believed that he knew then what he loved, whom he loved, and what was to become of him. He was not unhappy, and he must have been comforted by a discovery of great beauty — if you will allow, as I always have, that beauty is what makes us happy even in the knowledge of our certain demise.

"What then happened was bound to happen. Some of Von Rothbart's lieutenants, trained not to respect the prince — which was partially my fault — could not restrain themselves in the presence of so attractive a target, and disregarded his order. They pulled back their bowstrings. Three arrows traveled low over the water and lodged deep in the breasts of three swans.

"It was as if the prince himself were struck. Even the others, inured to the kill, grimaced at the sight of the swans dying in water reddened with their own blood. They died not only of their wounds, but, thrown off balance by the arrows, they drowned, rolling over without being able to right themselves, their long necks thrust downward.

"The prince's face tightened in an expression I have seen only in battle, and rarely even then. I knew that a violent act was about to occur, and that it was inevitable — as if he were not a man but a wave about to break or lightning about to uncoil from a thundercloud.

"He loaded the first arrow faster than anyone could see and

sent it into the heart of the first of Von Rothbart's lieutenants. Before the other could turn, his heart, too, was stopped forever. The third man let off a shot at the prince, who dropped to dodge it. It flew by us invisibly, but we could hear it. In one movement the prince rose, loaded another arrow, and plucked his bowstring. The arrow went straight to its target.

"Now the world had come apart, and the heart of the empire would divide in two, as the emperor had foreseen: Von Rothbart against the prince. Both were able and prepared. None of us standing there had any doubt whatsoever that the war would be long and terrible. In truth, as soldiers and former soldiers, we all expected to die.

"Stunned and immobile, we remained on the shore of the lake, overtaken by the amazement of having witnessed the separation of one era from another. It was as if highest summer had become darkest winter with the unexpectedness of a thundercrack in the snow.

"In the paralysis and confusion of the moment, the prince, now free, mounted and rode away. Several of Von Rothbart's men went after him. I myself stayed where I was, not knowing quite what to do."

"I hope it was the best ride of his life. I have often thought of what it might have been like, of what he might have been thinking and how he felt. I doubt that he was planning a rebellion. The clarity of those last hours must have allowed him to see that he had little chance of success — not because he wasn't able, but because his interests had turned elsewhere. All the while, when he was imprisoned at court, he had been growing and he had changed. To unseat Von Rothbart, he would have had to have become a general, to deal primarily with objective forces—strategy, logistics, and politics. But I am convinced that he had been conquered by the world of the heart and all the possibilities therein. He had seen that some small and seemingly powerless actions, or simple coalitions of light, sound, and color, can be supremely powerful in regard to the soul of a man, and can take him to other worlds. And he had seen that, though sometimes hidden, they exist in this world in legions, in armies, in multitudes. I am sure that when he saw the swans gliding around the point he apprehended another realm, as one sometimes does, and was ready to follow, far into oblivion, wherever it led in darkness or in light.

"With this resolution comes the greatest surge of freedom anyone can ever know. And if you couple it with an escape on horseback through the pines and meadows of a mountain forest in summer, with clouds moving in slow counterpoint across a field of azure, then perhaps you can imagine what he felt.

"I see the sharp ears of his Damavand horse bobbing in the wind as the roads and trails are rapidly consumed underneath. I see the evergreens flowing by, closing behind the prince and his horse in a wall of dark green like a wake. I feel the wind, the velocity, his sense of flying and rising.

"He may have known that Von Rothbart's men were close behind, for to follow him into the tighter curves and through the deepest part of the forest they would have had to have been close. He may not have cared, or perhaps he was unaware. Had he known what awaited him, I imagine, he would have turned to kill his pursuers.

"When he reached the hut, he did turn to look at them, and they stopped and rode away. Then he went inside. Imagine what he felt upon finding not only Odette but a small child in her arms — his own. And when he dismounted, the child's face lit up. Having a child to protect makes impossible the kind of metaphysics he was contemplating on his ride, the risks and glories and whatever they may require in regard to sacrifice and dying. With a baby to care for, you must be as prudent as a grocer. But he had already thrown down the challenge, and they were as deep in the forest as you can get, with nowhere to flee: other parts of the empire did not have the same kind of sheltering terrain.

"He had one day with the infant and Odette, during which he and Odette must have known what awaited them and their child."

"With a hundred and fifty of his best men, Von Rothbart left the city. Except for the Damavand warriors, weeks away, no formation existed with the power to counter them. The army was scattered in the disintegrating provinces, and, spoiled by irregular warfare in fixed positions, its cavalry had long before lost its edge. Even had a force to counter Von Rothbart's existed, I could not have mobilized it fast enough to have caught him. He would have had a considerable head start, and he was not going off to fight a battle, which might have offered delays, but to murder.

"I rode behind them, hoping that I would be able to warn the prince and Odette. But as I hadn't any idea of where the prince and Odette were, I could only follow. I dreamed of riding through Von Rothbart's ranks at the very last, but I knew that I was too old for such things, and that his soldiers would cut me down. I thought of stopping him with a shot from my bow, but I was not the bowman I once had been. Still, I followed relentlessly, with no more control of my forward career than if my horse and I had been falling off a mountainside.

"The soldiers hardly stopped in the clearing before the cabin. Instead, they made a wide turn and increased their speed. They had seen the prince and Odette at the top of a high meadow to the south.

"I wondered why the two of them were not mounted, and why they had gone to such an open place, where they were immediately observed. There, on foot, they had no chance whatsoever.

"This I simply could not understand until just after the soldiers had left the clearing, for then I saw an old woman dart from the cabin, with a baby swaddled in her arms. At first I was confused, but as they disappeared into the forest I understood everything, and I was so moved, and so proud of the young man I had raised, that I could hardly go on.

"But I had to go on. I rode up onto the meadow as fast as I could, so slowly, it seemed, that I wondered if I were dreaming.

"Von Rothbart did not dare approach the prince until his archers had dismounted and drawn their bows. Then he walked his horse ahead and halted. The prince and Odette were on the edge of a bluff so far above the lake that the lake's waves looked like a light coat of oil refracting the sunlight. This must have been where he had seen the swans rise in a gold-and-white column.

"When I arrived, the arms of the bowmen were quivering, their arrows set to fly. I was behind their line, but still close to my boy and Odette. He smiled at me as if to stay any action, as if to say that he was content, and as if to say goodbye. But how could he have been content, except perhaps in knowing that his child had escaped?

"I could do nothing against a hundred and fifty archers with their arrows aimed. The wind that rose from the lake, flowed over the cliff after its dizzying climb, and made Odette's home-spun dress luff at her ankles, carried her words to me. This was the first time I had seen her, and the last. She was very beautiful: you should know that. It is important for you to know that. She was in his arms, facing him, and she said, gently, 'I am afraid of nothing, but I cannot abide being killed by arrows.' Without realizing it, she had remembered her mother and her father.

"Then, with the saddest expressions I have ever seen, they looked into one another's eyes, held tight, and leaned into the wind. For a terrible moment we watched them fall, until they disappeared from view. May God forgive me if this is no more than an illusion that I myself have created, but they did not tumble or become entangled, they fell with what appeared to be increasing slowness. They fell as if they knew how to take to the air. They fell in smooth dampened curves that promised flight."

"When Von Rothbart wheeled his horse about in that meadow, he knew the empire was his. Though he would be censured for the death of the prince, he could justify it, and in truth he had not killed him.

"And as far as Von Rothbart knows," the old man said, turning to look the child straight in her eyes, "there are no heirs."

"But there are!" she exclaimed.

"Yes. There is an heir, who may someday return to claim a kingdom and an empire, though I am far from sure that this is what the prince and Odette would have wanted. Nonetheless, it will be up to their child to decide in what realms she will go."

"She?" the child asked, already deeply loyal to the rightful heir.

"She," he repeated.

"How do you know?"

The old man nodded before he spoke. "After the others were gone, I found myself in no condition to move. For an hour or so I remained above the lake, not daring to look down but instead trying to summon in my memory as best I could the image of those two young people. Every death that truly touches you hastens your own, and when it is the death of someone so young — well, for an old man like me, it is almost unbearable.

"I confess that in those moments I thought of joining them,

and I suspect that following them would not have been difficult. As I contemplated this, standing near the edge, I heard a whistling in the air, like that of powerful wings. The upwelling of the wind had brought the sound to me early. I dared not look, and I did not have to, for the sound was rising.

"I faulted myself for wishful thinking, and I told myself that even were I not imagining this sound, its significance would lie only in what I wished rather than in what was. There are certain great and beautiful things that to all appearances find defeat in this world. All proof, all reason, show them to have fallen, and as often as not our hope is merely our punishment. But in this world there are as well wrenching and great surprises that take us beyond what we can reason and what we can prove.

"I have merely my hope, but I have it still. I have not abandoned it, and will not. The sound was the sound of wings. They rose, and their whistling and beating on the wind grew so loud that it deafened me. I shuddered before they cleared the edge. They came on with great speed. They did clear the edge, and they filled the sky — two swans, wings extended, riding on the air and powering themselves ahead. They went right over me at great speed and disappeared beyond the trees as if they had a most specific and compelling destination. And I was left with nothing but the sound of wings echoing in my ears.

"Far away, on the crest of meadows leading into the high mountains, I saw the figure of the woman who had fled from the cabin. Though I would have to descend, and go around the lake, I knew I could reach her before dark, because my horse was a good horse."

The child, whom he loved so much, had begun to cry.

"I have always known, from the way that Odette remembered without memory, that, even without memory, their daughter would dream of finding them, and that she, too, would be loyal. But they are gone, and she cannot find them, except perhaps in the beating of her own heart, or when in the quiet of the forest a swan takes flight, and the white blaze of its wings brings them to life in her eyes."

Now she was sobbing. He took her in his arms and stroked her head. "You needn't grieve," he said, "for the story has come full circle, and you know the end. My horse was a good horse. I was able to reach them, on a high meadow, before dark — the woman and the infant child — and I have remained with them ever since."

Mark Helprin was raised on the Hudson and in the British West Indies. After receiving degrees from Harvard College and Harvard's Graduate School of Arts and Sciences, he did postgraduate work at the University of Oxford and served in the British Merchant Navy, the Israeli infantry, and the Israeli Air Force. He is a fellow of the American Academy in Rome. He sold his first story to the *New Yorker* more than two decades ago, and used the proceeds to buy a suit in the boys' department of Brooks Brothers. He has been a frequent contributor since, and his work appears as well in the *Atlantic Monthly*, the *New Criterion*, the *Wall Street Journal*, the *New York Times*, and many other publications here and abroad. He has won a PEN/Faulkner Award, the National Jewish Book Award, and the Prix de Rome. Translated into more than twelve languages, his books include A DOVE OF THE EAST & OTHER STORIES, REFINER'S FIRE, ELLIS ISLAND & OTHER STORIES, and WINTER'S TALE. Mark Helprin lives with his wife, Lisa, and two children, in "a forest overlooking the Pacific, from which come the sounds of foghorns, surf, and barking seals."

Chris Van Allsburg was born in Grand Rapids, Michigan. He entered the University of Michigan with vague ideas about becoming a lawyer, but sculpture courses convinced him that casting bronze would be more fun than filing briefs. He received his B.F.A. in sculpture in 1972 and an M.F.A., also in sculpture, from the Rhode Island School of Design. His art has been shown nationally in museums and galleries. In 1979, Van Allsburg published his first children's book, THE GARDEN OF ABDUL GASAZI, which was named a Caldecott Honor Book and a *New York Times* Best Illustrated Book of the Year. He has since won numerous children's book awards, including the American Book Award and two Caldecott Medals. Chris Van Allsburg lives in Providence, Rhode Island, with his wife, Lisa.

Designer: Susan Sherman
Manufacturing Manager: Donna Baxter
Type: Caslon 540 by Achorn Graphic Services, Inc., Composing Room of New England
Full-Color Illustrations: Case-Hoyt Corporation, printer
Paper: Patina Matte by S. D. Warren Company
Two-Color Text: Horowitz/Rae Book Manufacturers, Inc., printer
Paper: Glatfelter Offset High-Opaque by P. H. Glatfelter Company
Binding: Horowitz/Rae Book Manufacturers, Inc.